D1413658

YOU
ARE
AMAZING

Alexa Kaye

Andrews McMeel
PUBLISHING®

YOU ARE AMAZING

copyright © 2017 by Andrews McMeel Publishing.
All rights reserved. Printed in China. No part of this book
may be used or reproduced in any manner whatsoever
without written permission except in the case of reprints
in the context of reviews.

Andrews McMeel Publishing
a division of Andrews McMeel Universal
1130 Walnut Street, Kansas City, Missouri 64106

www.andrewsmcmeel.com

17 18 19 20 21 TEN 10 9 8 7 6 5 4 3 2 1

ISBN: 978-1-4494-8711-9

Library of Congress Control Number: 2016959653

You Are Amazing was first published in the United Kingdom
in January 2017 by Summersdale Publishers.

Editor: Patty Rice
Art Director: Holly Swayne
Production Editor: Erika Kuster
Production Manager: Tamara Haus

Image credits: Vector / E_K / NadineVeresk / Vanzyst
© Shutterstock

ATTENTION: SCHOOLS AND BUSINESSES
Andrews McMeel books are available at quantity
discounts with bulk purchase for educational, business, or
sales promotional use. For information, please e-mail the
Andrews McMeel Publishing Special Sales Department:
specialsales@amuniversal.com.

To.................

From.............

Introduction

When you're bombarded with challenges in life, it's easy to feel unsure and stop your true self from shining. But even when you're suffering from self-doubt, you can learn to release your fears and tap into the confidence you were born with. By consulting your own internal guidance and nourishing yourself with positive thoughts and emotions, you can boost your confidence and start to live life to the maximum. This collection of inspiring quotations and simple tips will help you to look on the bright side and remember that you deserve the very best in life, because you are amazing!

Let Go of Perfect

Remember that life is not like the movies. Although it can be very motivating to strive for that dream job, car, partner, or pair of shoes, when reality doesn't live up to your expectations it's easy to become disheartened. But there's no need to blame yourself. Doing the best you can, and making the best of what you have right now, is all that you need to do.

Do your thing
and don't care
if they like it.

TINA FEY

Write your own fairy tale. If you could create a "happily ever after" story of your life, how would it go?

....

....

....

....

....

....

....

Don't compare yourself with anyone in this world. If you do so, you are insulting yourself.

BILL GATES

Be Yourself

It's almost impossible to be yourself when you're constantly worrying what other people think. Let go of these concerns. The real you is the person you are when nobody is watching—when there's nobody you're trying to impress. Children are the experts at this. Notice how free they are, how they play and enjoy the moment. They dance and do cartwheels and don't care what people think of them. Ignore any inner clamoring for approval and embrace the real you! You'll have a lot more fun and people will be drawn to you as if by magic.

What great
thing would
you attempt if
you knew you
could not fail?

ROBERT H. SCHULLER

Imperfection is beauty,
madness is genius,
and it's better to be
absolutely ridiculous
than absolutely boring.

MARILYN MONROE

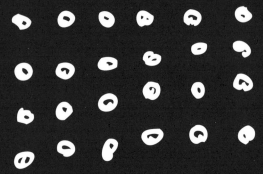

You can steer
yourself in
any direction
you choose.

DR. SEUSS

How would
your best friend
describe you?
Pick three words.

_____

_____

_____

Love Your Body

Your body is extraordinary. It is made up of 37 trillion cells, which all work as a team to keep you breathing, laughing, singing, and dancing. Your heart beats 100,000 times a day. Nerve impulses travel to and from your brain as fast as 170 miles per hour. The thousands of miles of blood vessels in your body could reach around the earth four times!

The next time you find yourself yearning to be taller, thinner, or firmer, take time to appreciate everything your body does for you. Love and cherish it—it's the most amazing thing you'll ever own!

If we all did the things we are capable of, we would literally astound ourselves.

THOMAS EDISON

Be yourself. The world worships the original.

INGRID BERGMAN

Express Your Individuality

There is only one you. Be proud of who you are and express your individuality. Daring to stand out means being your true self. It means dressing the way you want to dress. It means living how you want to live and sharing your gifts and talents with the world. It means following your dreams and standing up for what you believe in (even if this goes against the crowd). Celebrate yourself, just as you are. It's time to let your uniqueness shine!

YOU ARE A WARRIOR, NOT A WORRIER.

Optimism is the faith that leads to achievement. Nothing can be done without hope and confidence.

HELEN KELLER

CONFIDENCE
IS YOUR
SUPERPOWER.

Each of us is a unique strand in the intricate web of life and here to make a contribution.

DEEPAK CHOPRA

Live with Passion

You have a unique purpose that only you can fulfill. To find your purpose, follow your passions. What lights you up? What gives your life energy and meaning? When do you enjoy yourself so much that you lose track of time? Don't worry what other people think. Whether you love playing the drums, coaching your friends, or learning outdoor survival skills, find a way to do more of what you love. By experimenting and trying new things, you'll reconnect with what makes your heart sing. Get in touch with your passions and get ready to enjoy an awesome life!

To love yourself
right now, just as
you are, is to give
yourself heaven.

ALAN COHEN

Design your own coat
of arms, choosing
symbols and images
that represent your
unique strengths.

Be Your Own Greatest Friend

When you're faced with challenges in life, it's good to have the support of friends, family, or your partner. But it's also important to have your own internal support system. If you catch yourself in the middle of some nasty self-talk, ask yourself, "Would I say this to my best friend?" Then reframe your self-talk so that what you're saying to yourself is positive and encouraging. Be your own best friend and treat yourself with the love and respect you deserve.

To fall in love
with yourself is
the first secret
to happiness.

ROBERT MORLEY

Think of a challenge
you've conquered. What
did you learn about
yourself from that
experience?

_____

_____

_____

In dreams and in
love there are no
impossibilities.

JÁNOS ARANY

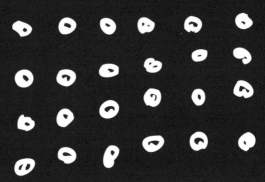

I think
confidence
is the sexiest
thing to have.

JESSIE J

Play Like You Mean It

Happy people are playful people! They are in touch with their sense of childhood joy and wonder. Think back to when you were a child. What did you enjoy doing? Did you love doing handstands, baking cookies, or riding your bike? Did you spend hours cloud gazing or making sand castles on the beach? Reconnect with that joy by making time to play again. Do things for pure fun: make a snowman, throw a Frisbee with friends, or play fetch with the dog. Let yourself be awed by the little things in life and see how your life changes.

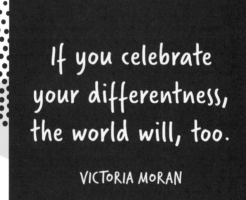

If you celebrate
your differentness,
the world will, too.

VICTORIA MORAN

YOU ARE AN
ADVENTURER
IN THE
GAME OF
LIFE!

Your attitude is like a box of crayons that color your world.

ALLEN KLEIN

Turn Failure into Success

Everyone makes mistakes from time to time: It's how you react to setbacks that matters. As long as you ask the right questions, failure can be a great teacher. Ask yourself, "What can I learn from this? What can I do better next time? What is this an opportunity for?" Don't let failure stop you—use it as a chance to grow and bounce back stronger and better than ever! Successful people know that failure is a stepping-stone toward success.

I have an everyday
religion that works
for me. Love
yourself first,
and everything
else falls into line.

LUCILLE BALL

Think about your perfect day, then draw or paint your vision. Which parts of your drawing can you start moving toward today?

With confidence,
you have won
before you
have started.

MARCUS GARVEY

Make Time for TLC

When did you last take time out to pamper yourself? A long, hot soak in a bath or a luxurious massage will melt away tension and show your hardworking body that you care. Holistic therapies such as reflexology and acupressure will replenish and restore you. Don't worry if you can't afford to book a treatment. There's a simple solution that's free: Ask your partner or a friend for a hug! Physical touch reduces stress hormones and releases oxytocin, leaving you feeling wonderfully warm and fuzzy inside.

Uniqueness is what makes you the most beautiful.

LEA MICHELE

The difference between ordinary and extraordinary is that little extra.

JIMMY JOHNSON

Small Steps

Is there an amazing dream buried deep inside of you? Don't keep it buried! Whether you long to sing on stage, run a marathon, or write a bestselling novel, honor that dream by taking small steps toward it. Research local singing teachers, go for your first mini jog, or jot down some titles for your book. The size of our dreams can sometimes overwhelm us. The solution is to face the fear and take action. Choose one small step you can implement today. It may mean stepping out of your comfort zone for a while, but living your dreams will light you up and fill you with a sense of direction and confidence.

Can you remember a
compliment that someone
paid you this week? How
did it make you feel?

———————————

———————————

———————————

The more you
like yourself,
the less you are
like anyone else,
which makes
you unique.

WALT DISNEY

GO GET 'EM,
TIGER!

Very little is
needed to make
a happy life;
it is all within
yourself, in your
way of thinking.

MARCUS AURELIUS

To be yourself in a world
that is constantly trying
to make you something
else is the greatest
accomplishment.

RALPH WALDO EMERSON

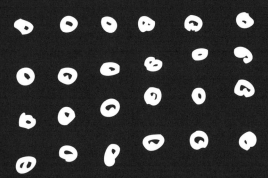

Let Go of Worries

Doubts and fears can sap your energy and hold you back. Free up some headspace by talking your worries through with someone close to you. Bringing a worry out into the light can make it easier to see the issue for what it is. After a few minutes you may wonder what you were so worked up about in the first place! If you don't have anyone to talk to at the moment, try downloading your thoughts and feelings onto paper. Draw a picture, reflect on your day, write a poem or song, or tie a note to a balloon and let it float away!

Beauty is
when you can
appreciate
yourself.
When you love
yourself, that's
when you're
most beautiful.

ZOË KRAVITZ

Is there an animal
you feel is a kindred
spirit? Fill this space
with photos and
drawings of this animal
and draw strength
from the images.

Believe in yourself!
Have faith in
your abilities!

NORMAN VINCENT PEALE

Be Mindful

Need a break from your busy mind? Slowing down and reconnecting with your body can help you reduce stress and embrace the present moment. Mindfulness is a great way to do this. Try walking barefoot on grass, focusing on the earth beneath your feet. Enjoy the sensation of water hitting your skin when you take a shower and notice how every inch of you feels alive. Go to a yoga class and see how it grounds you and gives you a sense of peace and calm. Reconnecting with your body will help you really savor life and all it has to offer!

Try to be like the turtle—at ease in your own shell.

BILL COPELAND

Man is most nearly
himself when
he achieves the
seriousness of a
child at play.

HERACLITUS

Revel in who you
truly are and
be liberated!

AMY LEIGH MERCREE

The most
beautiful thing
you can wear
is confidence.

BLAKE LIVELY

In what ways did you
surprise yourself this week?
Did you do something you
never thought you'd be
able to do?

_____

_____

_____

Use Your Imagination

Many people give up on their goals because they run out of drive and energy. However, there's a secret trick that will supercharge your motivation. Do what elite athletes do and visualize your success in great detail. Close your eyes and use all your senses to imagine how your outcome will look, feel, smell, taste, and sound. For this to work, you need to make the experience as vivid and real as possible. Where are you? Who are you with? How do you feel? Repeat this visualization exercise on a daily basis and use the energy and excitement it generates to propel you toward your dreams.

Put your ear
down close to
your soul and
listen hard.

ANNE SEXTON

INHALE CONFIDENCE. EXHALE SELF-DOUBT.

The essential lesson I've learned in life is to just be yourself. Treasure the magnificent being that you are.

WAYNE DYER

Tell me, what is it you plan to do with your one wild and precious life?

MARY OLIVER

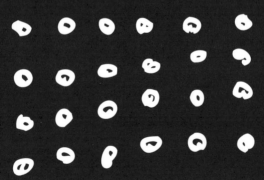

Please Yourself!

It's natural to want to be liked and accepted. However, excessive worrying about what other people think can stop you from stepping into your full magnificence! Remember, this is your life and only YOU know what's best for you. By focusing on your own internal guidance, rather than other people's opinions, you'll feel more at ease with yourself and others. This takes conscious effort and practice, but it's worth it. It's impossible to please everyone all the time, so relax. Make sure the number one person you please is yourself!

Write a list of ten things you love and appreciate about yourself and decorate it with hearts.

Fabulous Food

One of the best ways to feel good—both inside and out—is to nurture your body with nourishing food. Steer clear of highly processed fast food. Opt instead for whole foods that will soothe and calm you, such as fruits and vegetables, meat and fish, and nuts and seeds. Besides giving your body the nutrients it needs to function at its best, treating your body with the love and respect it deserves will give you a sense of strength and empowerment.

Life is either a
daring adventure
or nothing.

HELEN KELLER

SHOW UP AND SHINE!

You only get one
chance at life
and you have to
grab it boldly.

BEAR GRYLLS

Be a Possibilitarian

If you're feeling stuck, here's a neat trick to get you moving again: Ask yourself "What if?" Words have power. Asking a positive question like this encourages your brain to search for solutions. In contrast, closed statements such as "I don't know," "I can't," or "It's impossible" shut down your creativity—so you're far less likely to come up with an answer. The next time you're feeling stuck, repeat an encouraging "What if?" statement to yourself, such as "What if I could solve this?" or "What if there was an exciting solution to this?" These questions will fill you with hope and confidence, and encourage your self-belief to soar.

If you can just
be yourself,
then you have
to be original
because there's
no one like you.

 MARC NEWSON

Write a few words of
appreciation to your
body, thanking it for
all it does for you.

_____

_____

_____

STAND
TALL.

Whatever we expect
with confidence becomes
our own self-fulfilling
prophecy.

BRIAN TRACY

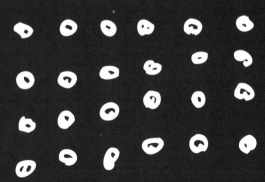

Train Your Brain

Did you know that gratitude makes you happier? It's been scientifically proven! An easy way to train your mind to notice the good things in your life is to write a gratitude list. Simply jot down three to five things you're grateful for every day—from small things such as a hug or a special note from a friend, to big ones such as a promotion at work or a fantastic vacation. Research shows that gratitude lifts our spirits by flooding our body with feel-good hormones. As you go about your day, actively look for people, places, and things that make your heart sing!

What you think, you become.

BUDDHA

Be unique.
Be memorable.
Be confident.
Be proud.

SHANNON L. ALDER

Honor
Your Needs

One of the best ways to love and care
for yourself is to honor your needs.
Tune in to what you most need right
now. Do you need a day off from study
or work? Would a bubble bath or an
evening curled up on the sofa watching
your favorite film soothe your soul?
Maybe you need a good belly laugh with
friends, a run on the beach, or a wild
night out? Whatever you need, put it at
the top of your to-do list. You deserve it!

Draw yourself
as a warrior. See
yourself as a strong,
confident person.

Give out what you most want to come back.

ROBIN SHARMA

The snow goose
need not bathe to
make itself white.
Neither need you
do anything but
be yourself.

LAO TZU

Aerodynamically the bumblebee shouldn't be able to fly, but the bumblebee doesn't know that so it goes on flying anyway.

MARY KAY ASH

Throw caution
to the wind and
just do it.

CARRIE UNDERWOOD

Declutter Your Life

Clutter can weigh you down and invite confusion and chaos, but you can breathe fresh air into your life by clearing out the clutter and creating an environment you love to be in. Tidy your study or work space, delete old files on your computer, and go through your wardrobe and throw out tired, worn clothes.

Once you're finished with your home, think about your life in general. Are you clinging to commitments, hobbies, or goals that no longer inspire you? Eliminating the clutter in your life will reduce your stress and make space for wonderful new things to come your way!

Always be a first-rate version of yourself, instead of a second-rate version of somebody else.

JUDY GARLAND

What dream(s) do you want to achieve? What would you do if you weren't afraid? Write down three things.

YOU ARE SO
AWESOME!

Breathe in Calm

Did you know there's a direct link between the way you feel and the way you breathe? Slow, deep breathing sends a message to the brain that everything is OK and it can calm down. The next time you feel stressed or anxious, inhale softly through your nose as your belly inflates with air, then breathe out s-l-o-w-l-y through pursed lips, as if you're blowing out a candle. Repeat this a few times and you'll activate the relaxation response in your body, leaving you feeling calm and centered.

Inner beauty
should be
the most
important part
of improving
one's self.

PRISCILLA PRESLEY

I often find it's just the confidence that makes you sexy, not what your body looks like.

QUEEN LATIFAH

Tension is who you think
you should be. Relaxation
is who you are.

CHINESE PROVERB

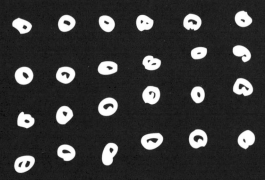

Life is a great
big canvas,
and you should
throw all the
paint on it
you can.

DANNY KAYE

Create your own personal Wall of Fame and write your accomplishments on it, whether small or large. Challenge yourself to list at least ten achievements that matter to you.

Beauty Is an Inside Job

The most beautiful people in the world are beautiful within. They love themselves and the world around them, and as a result, they exude confidence and charisma. Think about what you are projecting out into the world. Do you love and accept yourself? Do you carry yourself with confidence? Remember, confidence is simply a feeling of certainty that you are worthy and deserve the very best in life. Forget about trying to live up to unrealistic media images of perfection and focus on improving self-love and self-acceptance.

If you can express your soul, the rest ceases to matter.

HUGH MACLEOD

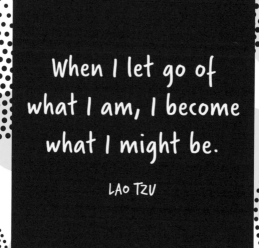

When I let go of
what I am, I become
what I might be.

LAO TZU

Your Own Vision Board

An awesome person like you deserves an awesome life! One way to make sure you achieve this is to create a vision board that includes pictures of all the things you want to do, be, and have. You can use photos, pictures from magazines, poems, motivational quotes, affirmations . . . anything that inspires and excites you. By placing your vision board where you can see it every day, you'll be constantly inspired and energized as you take steps toward creating your ideal life!

Beauty is a radiance that originates from within and comes from inner security and strong character.

JANE SEYMOUR

Who are your role models and heroes? Why do they inspire you?

....

....

....

....

....

....

....

....

Don't be afraid to go out on a limb. That's where the fruit is.

H. JACKSON BROWN, JR.

Affirm Your Amazingness!

Affirmations are a great way to boost your self-confidence. When you repeat a positive statement to yourself, you send a powerful message to your subconscious to think and behave in positive ways. Have fun "trying on" different affirmations or mantras until you find the right one. Home in on words and phrases that lift your spirits, even if they sound a bit silly! For example, "I believe in ME," "I am strong. I am invincible!" or "I am a star; this is my chance to shine!" Stand in front of the mirror and affirm your awesomeness every day. You'll be amazed at the difference it makes!

Believe with all
of your heart
that you will do
what you were
made to do.

ORISON SWETT MARDEN

It's just better to be yourself than to try to be some version of what you think the other person wants.

MATT DAMON

YOU ARE
UNSTOPPABLE!

Movement Medicine

The quickest way to feel good? Get off the couch! Studies show that 20 minutes of physical activity can boost your mood for up to 12 hours. Exercise is also one of the best ways to boost your body image and self-esteem. You don't have to be a gym rat. You could go to a Zumba class, go rollerblading with a friend, head to the community center for a swim, or join a basketball team. Whichever activity you choose, focus on the joy of moving your body, the exuberance of the music and/or the camaraderie of being with friends. Make sure you take your dose of movement medicine several times a week. Your confidence will be sky-high!

If you had all the time and money in the world, what would you do? How can you take small steps toward these things today?

. . . .

. . . .

. . . .

. . . .

. . . .

. . . .

When you're true to
who you are, amazing
things happen.

DEBORAH NORVILLE

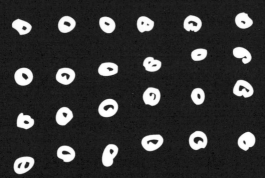

One way to get the most out of life is to look upon it as an adventure.

WILLIAM FEATHER

Adventure Is the Spice of Life

Adventures aren't just for millionaires who can afford to travel the world, jumping out of planes! An adventure is anything that's unique and enjoyable and that takes you away from your usual routine. With this definition, all you need for a life of adventure is a willingness to try new things. Daily adventures could include trying new foods, saying yes to meeting new people, signing up for an activity you've always wanted to try, or exploring an area you've never been to before. By saying YES to adventure you'll open your world to spontaneity, excitement, and new opportunities.

As soon as you start to pursue a dream, your life wakes up and everything has meaning.

BARBARA SHER

Believe and act
as if it were
impossible to fail.

CHARLES F. KETTERING

LIFE IS A ROLLER COASTER —ENJOY THE RIDE!

Who would you like to
thank in your life?
Write down their names
and why these people
are so special to you.

_____

_____

_____

Every day holds
the possibility of
a miracle.

ELIZABETH DAVID

Positive People

The people you spend time with can have a big impact on how you feel. Are you surrounded by positive, supportive people? Do you feel happy and optimistic after spending time with your friends? Build a community of positive people around you, so that you can nurture and support each other in times of need and get together to celebrate your achievements. Spending time with enthusiastic people who applaud your dreams will inspire you to be the best possible you!

Our entire
life consists
ultimately
in accepting
ourselves as
we are.

JEAN ANOUILH

Live life as though nobody is watching, and express yourself as though everyone is listening.

NELSON MANDELA

You, Unlimited

Life is precious and we only have one shot at it, so dream big! Don't put limits on what you can achieve. Walt Disney was fired from his job because he "lacked imagination and had no good ideas." Oprah Winfrey was told she was "unfit for television." Don't let others dictate your destiny. Nothing is impossible with belief and perseverance. From today, adopt some new beliefs that will support and empower you on your life journey, such as:

- "There is always a way if I'm committed."
- "I always find a way to overcome challenges."
- "I'm not afraid; I'm excited about what lies ahead!"

Your time is limited, so don't waste it living someone else's life.

STEVE JOBS

Draw yourself as a tree. The roots are where you've come from, the trunk is who you are today, and the branches and leaves are where you're going. How high and far will you reach, and what fruit will you bear?

Put your heart, mind, and soul into even your smallest acts. This is the secret of success.

SWAMI SIVANANDA

Wise Words

Do you have a favorite motivational quote or saying? Words of wisdom from great writers, philosophers, and thinkers can be a powerful source of inspiration. Best of all, they can be there for you whenever you need them! Start to collect inspiring books, poems, and quotes that you can dip into on a regular basis. You could even print out your favorite quotes and stick them on your wall or bathroom mirror—anywhere you will see them every day and their feel-good vibes can seep into your subconscious.

Growing old
is mandatory.
Growing up
is optional.

CHILI DAVIS

When you have a dream,
you've got to grab it
and never let go.

CAROL BURNETT

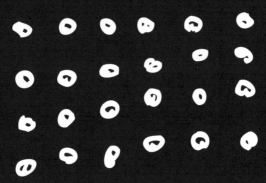

You have a treasure within you that is infinitely greater than anything the world can offer.

ECKHART TOLLE

Is there something you want to do but haven't had the courage to start? Write about how it would feel to begin this task and complete it!

· ·

· ·

· ·

· ·

· ·

· ·

The most effective
way to do it,
is to do it.

AMELIA EARHART

Play to Your Strengths

True happiness comes from loving yourself and embracing your strengths. Stop fretting over what needs fixing and focus instead on what you excel at! What gifts, skills, and talents do you have? Are you able to see the good in challenging situations or persist when other people give up? Perhaps you bake amazing cakes or are great with children? Many people base their sense of self-worth on external factors, such as how much money they earn or what other people think of them. However, rock-solid self-esteem comes from loving and accepting yourself just the way you are. Celebrate your talents and unique strengths.

Life is a helluva lot more fun if you say "yes" rather than "no."

SIR RICHARD BRANSON

YOU ARE THE CEO OF YOUR LIFE.

What's on Your Bucket List?

A simple exercise that can help you reconnect with what's most important to you is to create a Bucket List. This is a list of all the wishes, dreams, and moments of joy you want to experience in your life. What goals would you like to achieve? What new experiences would you like to have? Write everything down—the big and the small—and really have fun with this! Once you've made your list, read it often to remind you of what you truly desire. Then get out there and make these things happen.

If you ask me
what I came
into this life to
do, I will tell
you: I came to
live out loud.

ÉMILE ZOLA

In what ways do
you take care of
and show love
to yourself?

_____

_____

_____

What we need
is more people
who specialize in
the impossible.

THEODORE ROETHKE

The purpose of dancing—and of life—is to enjoy every moment and every step.

WAYNE DYER

Be Inspired

The world is full of inspirational people who are living life on their terms. Seek out role models who have overcome incredible odds to succeed. Listen to their words of hope and encouragement. You don't have to meet them in person. You can find them in the pages of a book and in TV interviews and documentaries. You can absorb their words of advice via their newsletters, videos, and blogs. Let their stories inspire you to embrace who you are and live the life you were destined to live!

Go confidently
in the direction
of your dreams.
Live the life you
have imagined.

HENRY DAVID THOREAU